This book is for those who have dreams of being rich. You know you'll never become rich working for somebody else; you only help make *them* rich—or more rich.

Your JOB pays the rent, clothes, utilities and a car that starts *most* of the time, and *maybe* you can save *some* money for your retirement years. Most of the time, there are two working in the same household and perhaps working two or more jobs. What can you do to change this? The ONLY answer is to . . . **GO INTO BUSINESS FOR YOURSELF!**

HOW, you ask? You have a family to feed so you have no money to invest. You can't go back to school; who *feeds* the family? Since you have little or no money, no bank will make a loan to you to start your own business.

You can make better than a good living in sales, but you're not a salesperson! And you don't have a college degree. You have no special skills because you've worked for someone else in some menial JOB most of your life. What CAN you do?

This book has the answers to **ALL** of those questions. It tells you HOW to be in business for yourself with no special skills, no college degree, and for very little money. Sounds unbelievable? It's TRUE!

# Anyone Can Do It!

# The

# New

# Millionaires

## Pyramid Schemes
## VS
## Home-Based
## Businesses

*EARN FROM:*
*$1,000 per month to $1,000,000 a Year*

by

# PETE BILLAC

Author: Pete Billac
Editors: Robin Houlette and Debra Merry
Layout Artist: Sharon Davis
Cover Design: John Gilmore

OTHER BOOKS BY PETE BILLAC:

The Annihilator
The Last Medal of Honor
How Not to be Lonely—TONIGHT
All About Cruises
New Father's Baby Guide
Willie the Wisp
Lose Fat While You Sleep
Managing Stress
The Silent Killer
Become an Internet Millionaire

Copyright @ August 2000
Swan Publishing
Library of Congress Catalog Card #00-106-4466
ISBN# 0-943629-46-2

THE NEW MILLIONAIRES is available in quantity discounts through: Swan Publishing, Southwind Ranch, 1059 CR 100, Burnet, TX 78611 e-mail: swanpub@tstar.net URL: http://www.swan-pub.com Phone: (512) 756-6800, Fax: (512) 756-0102

Printed in the United States of America.

In most books, this is the DEDICATION page. I wanted to use it to explain my *style* of writing. I write with words that are CAPITALIZED, *italicized*, **bold faced** and with "quotation marks." Since most of my books are in the *How-To* category, I want to make ABSOLUTELY certain that there is **no room** for even a *hint* of MISINTERPRETATION. Let me explain why.

As a kid in grade school, teachers said I had a fantastic memory; not smart, you understand—a good MEMORY. I *remember* a six-line example of how a single word—EMPHASIZED—changes the meaning of the entire sentence: I NEVER SAID HE STOLE THAT!

> I never said he stole that!
> I **NEVER** said he stole that!
> I never **SAID** he stole that!
> I never said **HE** stole that!
> I never said he **STOLE** that!
> I never said he stole **THAT**!

And THAT, my critics, professional writers, and English teachers who blast my writing style (most of whom have never written a best seller)is **why** I chose to put the *emphasis* on certain words. Just blame it on *my* "writing style" and go write your own book.

# FOREWORD

If you've wanted information on how you can start a home-based business, it's in this book. I say that YOU can earn $1000 a month to a MILLION dollars a year. How could I possibly promise **that**? Truthfully, most of you will NOT even come *close* to earning a million dollars a year. But you CAN, if you try, work TOWARD earning a million dollars; many have done it. More than 99% have not. So earn *half* that much. Or half **that** much. Or Even half THAT much. That's $2,000 a WEEK and you *can* do it. What I mean is YOU can do it! ANYBODY can!

It isn't *easy* to get rich. If it was, EVERYBODY would be rich. But I'll tell you what. There is (probably) NO CHANCE of your EVER being rich working for somebody else at a JOB. You simply HAVE to work AT YOUR OWN BUSINESS. You'll work harder, longer hours and have many stumbling blocks but so WHAT? I say TRY it and give yourself a CHANCE to make it. It might be your ONLY chance!

I'm *candid*, and sometimes almost *brutal,* because I'm after but ONE goal, and that is to help *you* become rich. And, I never mean to insult anyone but if I do, I apologize. I want to be your friend. You know that even your *best* friend won't always tell you the truth for fear of hurting your feelings; but I will— I'LL TELL YOU THE TRUTH and often there is no delicate way to do it.

This book "talks" to you in plain words. It tells the good and the bad about the very BEST way I've found for a *non-rich* person to become rich, and I go "*right for the jugular*" when it comes to your making money. I'd like you to enjoy your trip to a new and richer financial life and I WANT you to become rich.

I tell you about these illegal *Pyramid Schemes* along with a brief history of Network Marketing, Multi Level Marketing (*same church, different pew*) and put to rest what many THINK they know, but really DON'T!

I've researched this subject for over four decades and what I tell you is fact. I have nothing to gain by lying to you; I'm not trying to SELL you anything, just this book, and you already bought *it!*

Also, I became rich working for myself and I certainly couldn't have done it working for somebody else. I'll tell you *how* I did it, how others have and ARE doing it, and how YOU can do it IF you want it badly enough.

The *first* hurdle to jump is the confidence (or lack of confidence) that you have in **yourself.** "*If you think you can—or think you CAN'T—you're RIGHT!*" By "*telling it the way it is*" you can decide for yourself whether a home-based business if for you or not; some people CANNOT work for themselves.

My total "mission" is to help those of you who REALLY AND TRULY *want* to become rich. Too many others are doing it and if you follow the advice in this text, the only reason you WON'T make it is if you are lazy or you quit. Yes, this book goes *right at it!* Now, let's US go right at it!

Pete Billac

# TABLE OF CONTENTS

## WISHES AND WANTS

*If you merely WISH for something,
you wait and HOPE it happens.*

*WHEREAS...*

*If you truly WANT something,
you go after it until you get it!*

## Chapter 1
# PYRAMID SCHEME

I ask that you read this book with an open mind because it is well-researched FACT. Before we begin ANY of this, let me put one *giant dog to rest*; **NETWORK MARKETING IS NOT A "PYRAMID SCHEME!"** Whenever I hear someone blurt out these words, I know immediately that they just **don't know what they're talking about.**

Most HEAR the terminology and it's mostly an *excuse* for them *not* to try, and to stay in their present situation. Don't even waste your time to explain it to them; their mind is closed! LOAN them this book, get it back in a few days, and if they haven't read it, PASS THEM UP! *"You can't teach a pig to sing. You waste your time and aggravate the pig."*

Yes, despite what you say, no matter **what proof** or evidence you have, no matter how efficiently you **cover their objections**, they'll fight you tooth and nail because THEY KNOW! They got involved in either a TRUE Pyramid Scheme because they were greedy or stupid and to cover this, they will go to battle with you over it to cover THEIR error. Or, they *heard* about such things and *mistakenly* labeled ALL of these businesses erroneously.

Don't "fight" with them. Smile and walk away. Let them remain in their *financial quagmire,* never changing their life or lifestyle and just watch YOU do it.

You see, a *Pyramid Scheme* is what goes on around Christmas. It's when you get a letter in the mail from a well-meaning friend who asks that you send $100 CASH in an envelope to a person and address you've never heard of before, and if you do this, the next week you'll receive 15 or 25 letters in the mail, all loaded with money for you to keep—tax FREE. Greedy and a bit stupid, huh?

MANY will get "bumped" in the end because you're not SELLING anything; it's just people sending money to people and when it ends, (and it DOES) the poor saps at the **end** who sent their money get NOTHING back! That, by the way is against the law. THAT is a **PYRAMID SCHEME!**

This past Christmas I got one that wanted me to send two THOUSAND dollars in the mail. A week later, yet another one asked that I send TEN thousand in the mail with a "chance" to get $500,000 back! The TRUTH is, SOME people (the ones at the beginning and near the top) DO make a lot of money but the folks on the bottom lose.

People who THINK they can make this easy money usually LOSE the hard-earned money they sent, HOPING to make a lot of money FAST and ILLEGALLY; they know, deep in their heart and soul, that SOMEBODY will NOT get paid, and when they first get involved, they KNOW its illegal, they KNOW it's a scam, yet they still do it. They deserve to be one of those at the bottom who lose.

Now, let's talk about what COULD be termed, a LEGAL pyramid and in NO WAY is it easy. It's *hard work*, very hard work, but it IS a CHANCE to make a lot of money and FASTER than any other way I know.

## MULTI-LEVEL MARKETING

One of the first Multi-Level Marketing companies most are aware of was *Shaklee;* they began in 1956. They were followed by *AmWay* (the most well-known) in 1959. Then came an outpouring of like companies including *Nature's Sunshine, Forever Living, Herbal Life, NSA Nutritional's, Mary Kay*, etc., etc., etc.

There is a "bad rap" running rampant in the entire WORLD that tells of people losing money, being GYPPED in a "Pyramid Scheme" and those who truly DON'T KNOW WHAT THEY'RE TALKING ABOUT who are so OPPOSED to these methods of making money SPOIL THE CHANCES of many.

No matter how well-meaning these folks are, their total MIS-information and MIS-conception of Network marketing as a PYRAMID SCHEME is entirely WRONG! THEY are wrong! Their ideas of Network Marketing are WRONG! Hopefully, this book will set them straight and if NOT, don't YOU fall prey to their negative ideas that are totally UN-founded!

In listening to these people who are AGAINST Network Marketing, ask them WHY? Were THEY in such a company? Or did they just HEAR of such happenings? Did THEY work? Did they QUIT? Did THEY pay the price of time and effort? Did they LEARN? Or did they try it THEIR way? Did they

REALLY give it a try or just "play" with it? Here's how much of this mess began.

MANY who worked as *distributors* in these beginning Multi-Level Marketing companies made BIG money and, as seems natural, some of them went into one form or another of these businesses for *themselves,* most failing miserably. You see, just because you can FLY a plane doesn't mean that you can BUILD one, or run an aircraft manufacturing *plant.*

The majority of these start-up companies failed in the very first year. **SO WHAT'S NEW?** The fact is, **MOST** new companies fail the first year but nobody knows about them except your family, your banker, and a few creditors.

Whereas, if you've built up a long list of DIS-TRIBUTORS that numbers in the tens and hundreds of **thousands,** the "word" gets out quickly and is widespread, and the disappointed distributors moan and groan and gripe and EVERYBODY "hears" bad things about the Multi-Level Marketing business and **MIS**-label it a PYRAMID SCHEME!

Those who started these companies didn't *mean* for them to fail, but they didn't have the EXPERI-ENCE or expertise. Many ran out of money, and in any new business you WILL make mistakes and only MONEY can help you "weather the storm." Also, MANY companies did *too* well, and THIS caused their demise. Doesn't make much sense that a company does well and STILL loses, does it? I'll explain.

I researched over 150 companies that went into the MLM business between 1960 and 1970 that grew *so quickly* there was NO WAY they could keep up with the new distributors that came pouring in. Records were messed up, orders were never taken or delivered, and the company closed. MUCH of the time the officers lost all of their investment money along with the distributors. But the multitude of distributors were hurt and thus, BAD PUBLICITY for MLM.

It's a well-known fact that when you PLEASE people, they tell their friends. When you DIS-please them, they tell *everyone they meet*—FOREVER!

From 1975 on, when the computer became a new way of doing business, record keeping was easier and companies could handle the *paperwork,* but many could not get the GOODS delivered. They couldn't *get ammunition to the troops.* Let me explain this.

Let's suppose the company was marketing a product like *vitamins.* The first month the fledgling MLM company sold 1,000 bottles and they bought these vitamins from a manufacturing source. And the second month they sold 3,000 bottles of vitamins and delivered *them.* The third month, when the sales grew to *ten* thousand bottles, the plant itself had trouble keeping up with the demand.

When distributors and sales DOUBLED in the fourth month (as many do) the plant had to put workers on around the clock to keep up. Then the *next* month the orders doubled again and the same the next month. Now, they were behind and by the time they bought more equipment and trained more workers, they were so backlogged that the company they were supplying (the MLM company) folded.

Yes, business was so GOOD that they couldn't

supply the demand; then what? They went bankrupt. You need to get "*ammunition to the troops.*" It was a classic case supply and demand—or rather, lack of supply. This resulted in MORE bad publicity for the MLM industry.

All the time there were new payment plans being devised to "beat the competition." Many of these well-meaning entrepreneurs began with the WRONG compensation plan, one they couldn't possibly survive with if they kept, so they CHANGED the plan and this, almost always, took money AWAY from the distributors.

The ones who were making BIG money stayed in because they had never made so much money in their lives, but it was the "little" folks who suffered. They had perhaps worked their way up to $3000 or $4000 a month and had QUIT their regular job. When *their* income was cut in half, or 30% or 20% was taken away from money they NEEDED to pay their bills, they couldn't survive and either went back for their old JOB, found a new JOB for less pay, or they went bankrupt.

Then, of course, when the "little" folks left, the BIG income earners, in the following months, saw an additional drop in *their* paychecks and they, too, had to look for another source of income. AND, when NOBODY is working, the company fails. When this happened, it set hundreds of thousands of tongues wagging about how the distributors were *scammed*! There was no SCAM! This was no "pyramid" that toppled, it happened the ways I pointed out. It's just life. It happens to new companies every day.

I watched and listened to the moans and groans

of distributors who THOUGHT they could make a fortune and were on their way to doing it when the COMPANY folded, and it *was* devastating to many. Especially those who told their boss *"to take his job and shove it"* (Johnny Paycheck song), only to have to go back, hat in hand, and ask for the job again. If they got their old job back (IF), what are their chances for a raise or promotion, huh?

I mention these painful experiences because many who have worked in the "wrong" business or with the "wrong" company, or sold the "wrong" product know what I mean. You worked hard, you had dreams that were shattered, but you came BACK, didn't you? We ALL learn from our mistakes—hopefully.

As time passed and Multi-Level Marketing was dubbed a "pyramid scheme" the name was changed to NETWORK MARKETING and now, we like to call it a HOME-BASED BUSINESS.

It's SAD to have to *change a name* because of TOTAL MISCONCEPTION by many, because Network Marketing (or whatever you choose to call it) made more MILLIONAIRES in the 20 past years than ANY OTHER industry in the history of mankind! And MOST of these folks started AT HOME, with a SMALL investment, and began "trying it" PART time!

## NETWORK MARKETING

I feel I should EXPLAIN to the unknowing and disbelievers exactly HOW Network Marketing works. Oh, I'll not convince EVERYONE of the legality and authenticity of this money-making business no matter WHAT I say because there are those who simply REFUSE to listen to reasoning; their mind is MADE UP! Don't fear; I'll *WHACK* at them throughout this book, because they are WRONG!

I think the *easiest* way to explain Network Marketing is people talking with people, who talk with people, who talk with people, who talk with more people, etc. It's a whole line of people **telling** people about the product(s) or services they represent.

There are *networking* clubs and organizations in just about every city in the WORLD where people meet and help each other sell or MARKET their wares through this NETWORKING; people telling people.

It is a LEGITIMATE home-based business and a way to work for yourself and earn extra money. I'd like to see EVERYONE at least TRY it if they want or need more income. You KNOW you need to work for yourself to make any BIG money.

With a *home-based business;* you **are** working for yourself. This means you don't need a store, newspaper or televison ads, or employees. It isn't necessary to drive to and from work, wear special clothes, or even *bathe* if you don't want to. Some of the most successful network marketers I've met never leave their homes. They DUPLICATE their system and themselves.

## DUPLICATION

A simple way to demonstrate how this *duplication*

method works is when we find a person who is hired to dig postholes for a large fence company. He is paid $10 a hole. No matter *how hard* or *how fast* he works, it seems that 10 holes per day was his maximum. The most he could ever expect to earn was $100 a day. And, the company needed more holes dug for more fenceposts to remain in business.

So, this enterprising young man found five of his friends who needed a job and he hired *them* to dig holes for **$9** each. He showed them how to do it; he DUPLICATED himself. He still earned his $100 a day digging his own holes, but **also** $10 from each of his five employees or $50 a day extra from them. They did the same as he.

They each found five people (25 total) who were digging 10 holes a day for **$8** a hole. NOW, he earned his same $100 from his efforts, plus he was taking in $50 from his five workers, and he was NOW getting **another** $1 a hole times 10 holes from 25 workers or TWO HUNDRED AND FIFTY DOLLARS per day from *their* efforts.

To take it one step further, each of THOSE 25, hired five people each (jobs weren't plentiful then) to dig the same holes for $7 a day. Want to figure that out? I'll do it for you. He had 125 more hole-diggers earning him an additional $1 per hole times 10 holes or TWELVE HUNDRED AND FIFTY DOLLARS PER DAY! THAT is how "duplicating yourself" earns you big money. THAT is the theory of Network Marketing!

That little beginning hole-digger with NO money, just DUPLICATION, needn't dig **any more holes**. His job, then, was to *watch over* the diggers, *cheer them on,* and replace the LAZY ones or those who quit. He was taking in more than FIFTEEN HUNDRED DOL-LARS a day! He began working *hard* and graduated to working *smart.*

Can it go on FOREVER? WHAT does? How long CAN it go on? What I mean is how many people can dig these holes until you are OUT OF PEOPLE?

Well, first of all, this is a fast example of how Network Marketing works. In reality, you run out of *holes to dig* faster than you run out of people to dig them. And you can't rush down in increments of $1 per hole, but sometimes on only 10 cents per hole. But, with enough people, those DIMES PER HOLE add up *astronomically.* Here's another, almost unbelievable example of duplication.

Whether you play golf or not is unimportant; just know that there are 18 holes on a regulation course. Let's say someone talks to you about making a wager on a game. You agree to start with betting a PENNY on the first hole, doubling the bet all the way through. Seems safe enough, right?

---

**The LAST HOLE plays for over
THIRTEEN HUNDRED DOLLARS!**

---

Don't believe it? Check it with your calculator. That, my friends, is the power of DUPLICATION and NETWORK MARKETING. That is how YOU can become rich if you work hard *and* smart. That's what I'm going to share with you in this book. Read and learn. It could make you wealthy, or at the very least, change your lifestyle to where you never have to read that menu *from right to left* ever again.

If you're the cautious type, work at it **part time.** In fact, I URGE you to try it part-time, ESPECIALLY if you are new at this because it takes some time to learn to do it correctly. Then, when you start earning *three times* more than you are making at your present job—for more than six months (maybe three or four months)—and you enjoy being in business for yourself, *quit* that regular job and do this full time.

## HOW YOU GOT INVOLVED

Usually, it's when you are first *dragged* by a friend or relative to one of these "opportunity" meetings and there is some silver-tongued devil telling how you can earn $10,000 up to $50,000 a month (or more) in *this* company if you follow directions and work at it a few hours per week.

WOW! This sounds great. *"I can work three hours a week and get rich,"* you tell yourself. The fact is, this HAS happened—but rarely! Don't count on it! What **I'M** telling you is to plan on about 30 or **35** hours a week IF you want to give yourself the best *chance*. Don't depend on LUCK. Make your OWN luck!

I've watched and researched these companies for over FORTY YEARS. About 1 to 3% earn in the mid six figures ($300,000 to $600,000 per year) and maybe 5 to 8% more earn a bit less, some above and around $100,000 in a year, about 10% make $500 to

$1,000 a week and the rest (about 80% make expenses, nothing, or *lose money*. These are FACTS!

So WHAT'S NEW, eh? So you blame THE COMPANY? Let's get real; 80 to 90% of those in ANY business—in **LIFE**—are **Un**successful! There is NO DIFFERENCE with those who "make it" as opposed to the ones that DON'T make it in Network Marketing. The ONLY difference is that you're in business for YOURSELF, that you have the OPPORTUNITY to get into that 20% or 10%—1 to 3% even—whereas with a JOB, you have almost NO chance. ALSO, you have a CHANCE to make it in only a YEAR or two.

Only a few percent of the people in the WORLD are rich or near rich and of course more people LOSE money than make money in *most* first-time businesses because they QUIT, that don't have the money to "hang on," or they are just not MEANT to be in business for themselves for any other number of reasons. Don't blame the Network Marketing industry for *worldwide* failure.

It's no different if you fail in any business, but in Network Marketing you have someone *else* to blame other than yourself. If you REALLY want a CHANCE to make big money, you simply HAVE to be in business for yourself. Network Marketing, to me, is the least expensive and easiest way to do this. If I went busted today, tomorrow I'd jump into Network Marketing!

If you will, especially those of you with this "Pyramid Scheme" mind set, please, read this book with an *open mind* and forget what you've heard from others, or a failure or two you experienced in the past. You made a MISTAKE! The COMPANY made a mistake! Remember, "**It isn't how many times you get knocked DOWN—It's how many time you GET BACK UP" that counts!**

## YOU FAILED IN THE PAST

If you *have* tried Network marketing and failed, perhaps you're not right for Network Marketing. Or you made some very *unwise* decisions from the onset. The tough part is having to tell your SPOUSE that you'd like to try *again!*

I see it EVERY DAY with people who have to "sneak" around their wives (or husbands) to work a business because they failed before and their spouse doesn't "back" them up. Many threaten a DIVORCE if their spouse tries it ONE MORE TIME! A BETTER chance for success is when both work together...in ANYTHING!

Lets's begin with those who were in Network Marketing two or three times (or more) and failed at it. Just to start with a clean slate, let's try to determine *which* of the following errors you were guilty of:

❖ **You became involved with the wrong company**
❖ **You tried to market The wrong product**
❖ **You were lazy**
❖ **You quit too soon**
❖ **You didn't take time to learn**
❖ **You wanted to work YOUR system**
❖ **You aren't bright enough to run your own business**

See? I WARNED you that I was candid and that I'll tell you "like it is." LOOK at these above reasons for failure (you were not ALWAYS to blame) and see which category(s) fit you. YOU decide.

Did you notice that EACH reason I say you failed started with Y-O-U? Look at them again. Is the COMPANY the culprit? Truthfully, SOMETIMES the company IS! As I said in the beginning of the chapter, many times the company closes because of inexperience or lack of funds, but MOST of the time it's because of the DISTRIBUTORS. Let's look at that angle and see if you agree.

## DISTRIBUTOR'S CLOSE MOST COMPANIES

If *any* company has 50,000 or 100,000 or more representatives, the chances are high that there will be some *fruit cakes* or *fast-buck artists* in the bunch, you know, those who try to beat *the system*. Since many of the top Network Marketing companies are in health care products like vitamins, herbs, or diets, their distributors OFTEN cannot follow the rules. They embark on *overkill* and LIE about or MISREPRESENT their product to make it more appealing to a consumer, and the *company* is held responsible for their actions and gets closed down.

Most (maybe ALL) NM companies **will not allow** their distributors to place an ad, make a statement to the newspapers, conduct radio or televison interviews, do their own newsletters, or go on the Internet because THEY SAY STUPID THINGS that *could* get the FDA or Attorney General's office or any number of agencies against the company, and the COMPANY is closed down! EVERYONE suffers.

How can you stop this? **YOU CAN'T!** It's human nature, and *Murphy's Law* comes into play often. I've seen (recently) several *promising and large* NM companies close their doors or lose 75% or more of their distributors because of some dumb and greedy DISTRIBUTORS who want to do it "their" way. They want an EASIER way, they want a FASTER way, and THEY mess up a company and ALL the other distributors in that company.

Each Network Marketing company sets down firm RULES on what a distributor can and can't do. They are CONSTANTLY either warning these rules-breakers or putting them OUT of the company. Still, it goes on all the time. And even if the COMPANY punishes or dismisses one of their distributors, and even though these governmental organizations KNOW the company, itself, is not guilty of wrongdoing, they shut them down!

## OTHER CAUSES FOR FAILURE

The COMPANY changes their policies, their marketing plan, they have fewer meetings, they begin to charge MORE for the product or service, MORE for the sales aids, MORE for company-held meetings and that, ultimately, is *goodbyeville* for that company. Nobody said only SMART people run these companies.

There is NO GUARANTEE with ANY company, and ALL companies have at least ONE corporate officer who is a *jackass,* and this never helps public relations or instills confidence in distributors. Where they come from and how they get there is beyond me, but I've seen it happen over and over.

Again, it happens in everyday life. You've all seen it with bankers, politicians, leaders of industry and you wonder HOW IN THE HELL DID THAT PERSON GET IN THAT SPOT? Sooner or later, hopefully, that "spot" will be filled with another person.

Companies experience buyouts, hostile take-overs, changes in management, in policy, etc. There is NO DIFFERENCE in Network Marketing companies than what goes on in other companies. Here's another reason.

When you are a State Attorney General and you are making $60,000 a year after graduating from college and then finishing law school, it's not an *easy pill to swallow* to learn of a retired schoolteacher, a garbage truck driver, or some former pizza delivery boy who are all making $400,000 a year in Network Marketing.

So, they go over your marketing plan with a fine toothed comb (it's their job, anyway) and if there is a *hint* of illegality, they move in and shut you down. That happened often a decade and more ago. Now, there are attorneys who specialize in setting up Network Marketing companies and this rarely happens.

In the back of the *contract* you sign (perhaps printed in small letters because they have a lot to say and limited space to do it) there is a clause that states "*The company has the right to change their compensation plan (even some of their rules) whenever THEY choose*" (or something to that effect). This means that the COMPANY, if their officers so vote, can CHANGE your pay without you having anything to say about it!

If this happens *after* you are involved, working and making money, you have two choices; *stay in or leave.* I've seen this occur many times with companies who either didn't know what they were doing and *had* to change their pay plan (rarely in *favor* of the distributors), or go out of business. Or, the company gets *greedy*, wants more, and ends up causing the entire organization to crumble.

## HARD, COLD FACTS

Remember, too, that you are an *Independent Distributor* and in business for yourself. They care about you as long as you are making money for *them*. Like a ball player, when their usefulness to the "team" is over, they are traded, sold, fired and/or forgotten.

Think *corporate* gives *one thought* about their distributors? Some do, and I've written books about the ones "I believe" are sincere and truly care, but don't be *naive*. **It's a business!** It's SURVIVAL! MOST corporate bigwigs tell you they care, but chances are they'll never see you again because you are out struggling to survive and they are living well.

I have a neighbor, Nolan Ryan, one of the best pitchers ever to play the game of baseball. When he was with the *Houston Astros,* he had the lowest ERA in the league but he lost too many games and did not win the *Cy Young* award as the best pitcher for that year. You see, *management* didn't get the players who could *hit* the ball, and Nolan would have had to pitch a *no-hitt*er to even tie. Sometimes he gave up two or three hits and LOST the game. Sometimes, *one* hit.

And management let him go to the Texas Rangers where he went on to pitch a few more *no hitters* and end up in the Baseball Hall of Fame. Management is for management. Smile, be friendly with them but look out for *yourself.* It's BUSINESS!

Let's suppose somebody comes in and points a gun at several of you and says "I'm going to kill TWO of you and the rest will live. *Which of you will it be*?"

This is an extreme example, but just know that most of you will get *whiplash* or *throw your arm out of socket* pointing at each other. And if *corporate* is in the group, think they will say "choose me?" YOU wouldn't either. I TOLD you I "tell it like it is!"

Conversely, if *you* get a better deal, *you* are gone, too. So *your* loyalty is to *your* business, and to yourself, and to YOUR family; their loyalty is to theirs. That's life as it is and not for the dreamers, idealist, or the *naive*.

BUT, on the *positive* side, If you worked hard, learned, trained, and have faith in your *own* ability and truly CARE for others, you'll rebound. You'll MAKE it happen. YOU'LL be financially independent on *one* of these tries. Remember, "*If you never Take a chance, you never HAVE a chance!*" You must take these setbacks in stride and persevere! If it was easy, we'd ALL be rich.

## COMPETITION

No matter WHAT you invent, concoct, formulate or discover, SOMEBODY will try to **COPY CAT** it and sell it cheaper, get it to you faster, promise a better pay plan, or offer more amenities and you go for it. It happens every day.

I remember the *Health Rider*, that rowing-type exercise machine that you sit on and exercise using your own body weight. A friend of mine, Lloyd Lambert, invented it. It sold for about $500 and *Covert Bailey*, best-selling author of *Fit or Fat*, was their primary spokesman. The company made a fortune.

Within minutes of the *first* TV campaign, about five *other* machines appeared on the market, some selling for less than $100. The hundred-dollar model wasn't as sturdy or attractive, but it sold and hurt the *Health Rider* sales immeasurably. But, the *Health Rider* survived because it is a quality item.

This happens in ALL businesses. If somebody else has the *same thing* that is cheaper (or *almost* the same thing) most people go for IT! What I'm asking you to do is to WEIGH out your options *before* going for it. That is why I say to choose a NM company who has a UNIQUE product that nobody can copy or sell cheaper, and go with them.

Yes, it's sometimes a tough world we live in with competition always nipping at our heels trying to ruin a good thing. We just have to be able to make the right decision and go on with our lives.

I know there could be other (personal) reasons for your failure other than these, but these are sufficient for you to get the idea. This book teaches you how to choose the RIGHT company, the RIGHT product, *and* how to really EARN money.

Now, let's find out how to give YOU the best CHANCE of making this fascinating business work for you!

**If you truly WANT something
you have never had,
you must be willing to DO something
you have never done.**

I don't want to supersaturate you with these "sayings" but some, are REALLY meaningful. I recite and recall to memory several from time to time.

## Chapter 2
# HOW MUCH CAN YOU EARN

This, of course, is impossible to tell because we're all different. How much TIME are you willing to put into this new business? How much STUDY? And how much EFFORT?

These are three important questions to ask yourself and, even then, you must know that there is no GUARANTEE! Even if you're honest with your self-appraisal, nobody can tell you what you can make. I can, however, give you a few *examples* of what OTHERS have done and then, it's up to you.

ANYONE can make big money in Network Marketing. I know (and know *of*)hundreds of people who are making a quarter of a million dollars a year with a Network Marketing company who have worked it far LESS than one year. Match THAT with a college degree—in almost anything?

And remember, I'm not trying to *sell* you anything or interest you into joining my company; **I have no company!** My business is writing books. I'm just trying to give you the secrets of making big money in an industry that gives you the *opportunity* to do it. I research a company like *Columbo*, then write about it. I'm not paid by any company, I don't SELL anything for any company, I don't BELONG to any company, nor do I RECRUIT for any company!

Whew! Now that *that* is behind us, I'd like you to tell me who *you* know who is earning $250,000 a year or more—*legally*—without a college degree, marrying into it, playing sports, being in the movies, winning the lotto, or who began their business with less than $500 and who hasn't been working most of their life at the same business.

I interviewed a former PIZZA DELIVERY BOY who, within ONE year, is now earning about $40,000 a month in Network Marketing! I met a *blind lady* who is 83 years old and she is earning about $8,000 a month in her Network Marketing company after seven months. And a young man 37-years-old who SAVED his parents' ranch in Canada by getting involved in an *Internet* marketing company. The ranch had been in the family for four generations and it was about to go into foreclosure and the son, in eight months, was earning $50,000 a WEEK!

That's right, $50,000 a WEEK; I checked it out and when I reached him I found that he lied. His check THAT week was **fifty SIX thousand**! Now I've *lost* many of you because you say this could not BE. Well, it IS!

Then another person I visited and SAW a weekly check (I call him "the alien" in one of my books because in every one of these companies there is one or two who, for WHATEVER reason, make more money than they can count) and I'm going to visit him at his MILLION-DOLLAR home in Australia in a few months. His secret? HARD, SMART WORK!

He saw the opportunity (he saw the PICTURE) with this one company and he went at it. He put in 16 to 18 hours a day, seven days a week for only six MONTHS and he earned a bit over **TWO million dollars** his first year. THIS year he stands to make as much as SIX million dollars (US)! Oh, I know those of you who earn a living working hard don't *really* believe me now, and I understand. It's difficult to believe that this is possible, BUT IT IS and—I SAW THE CHECKS!

There are dis-believers EVERYWHERE! DON'T LISTEN TO THEM! DON'T let their unknowing opinion *dissuade* you from a CHANCE to earn a lot of money. To have a college degree, get a JOB for a bunch of years, support a family, go to work on time and never miss but a few days in your LIFE, and in the good years earn maybe $100,000 only to find out that a high-school dropout PIZZA BOY is earning that is less than three months has to "rub you wrong."

Had I not researched the Network Marketing industry, had I not SEEN and WITNESSED fortunes being made, my feelings would be hurt, too. I worked HARD many years of my life. I grunted and sweated and made little money MANY times. I did "floor" and "tower" work in oil fields while going to college.

I worked as a LONGSHOREMAN on the Mississippi in New Orleans at night and taught school during the day to support a wife and daughter; got off school at three, made it home, wolfed down food and got in "old" clothes and was at work by five, and worked until 1 am, bathed, slept five hours and did it all again.

During high school, my "fun summers" were spent in the hot sun, but not on a beach. I worked on a road gang building a highway through the swamps of Louisiana with mosquitoes, water moccasins and alligators and stifling heat as constant companions.

One summer I chipped paint from the hull of a *rustbucket* cargo ship bound for Africa. When we got there I was *half* done, and the other half I did on the trip back. The very WORST job, I recall, was when I agreed to cut some miserable old lady's vacant lot for six-dollars. I'll NEVER forget that experience. It took me three DAYS working 12 hours a day in HOT sun.

The weeds were high and when I agreed to cut them, I never KNEW that inside the *first row* of high weeds were about 500 RAILROAD TIES and cement blocks that had to be moved and stacked BEFORE I could cut the weeds and MOW it (hand mower in those days—no motor).

I remember straining and pushing and rolling and shoving those things that got heavier as that merciless sun beat down on me. But she *did* offer me iced tea—14 glasses; she kept count. I got my six dollars MINUS 42 cents because she CHARGED me three cents per glass for the damned tea! I *never* forgot *that* lesson. Ever since then I do RESEARCH and ASK QUESTIONS **before** I make a major decision—well, *most* of the time.

Those are just a few examples of working hard and not earning much money. A MILLION dollars? There wasn't that much money in the WORLD! That was only for the Rockefeller's, and the Ford's, and the Whitney's, and the Vanderbilt's! I'd have settled for a thousand dollars for the entire summer working ANY of those jobs. On the job I'll never forget, I'd have been happy to have my 42 cents back for the tea.

Of *COURSE* it upsets those who work so darn hard to see a former pizza delivery boy earning half a MILLION dollars a year (without even a high-school diploma), or a grass cutter, an auto mechanic, or a GARBAGE TRUCK driver! Most just do NOT believe it! I can't blame them for thinking that, and "I see where they're coming from."

*"This doesn't happen to everybody,"* the cynics will say. **Of COURSE it doesn't!** But it happens to MANY and it is not LUCK. Luck has little to do with most successes. Keep an open mind, work SMART, put in the time, and make your *own* luck. If you see an OPPORTUNITY, a CHANCE to change a life of "want," and it LOOKS reasonable and doesn't cost much to TRY, I say GO FOR IT!

*A.J. Foyt*, famous race car driver and four-time Indianapolis 500 winner who lives but a few miles from me, said; *"LUCK, is when opportunity meets preparation."* You make your own luck. If you are able to recognize an opportunity and it looks like it *might* work for you, give it a try.

I know a husband and wife team who were both school teachers for over 20 years and their first year in Network Marketing they earned over $600,000. I know yet another husband and wife team (she's a former schoolteacher, too) who are at about $75,000 a WEEK in a Network Marketing company they have been in about 10 months.

This DOES happen to many! It isn't EASY; if it was easy, EVERYBODY would be rich. It's HARD work! It's MANY hours! It's SMART work! It's sacrifice that MOST are unwilling to give. It's never quitting! It's choosing the right company and the right product that YOU feel you can become successful working.

I could go on and on with more testimonials but, *phooey* on them, they're making it. Let's talk about YOU and how YOU can do the same or better. Is it REALLY possible! **YES, it is!**

All *you* have to do is be willing to learn, put in the time, and work hard AND smart. Hard work is great and you'll earn *some* money working hard no matter how many mistakes you make. But SMART work is better. And, hard, smart work simply cannot fail— IF you have the right vehicle.

## WHAT TO LOOK FOR

At least three times a week I am called, faxed or e-mailed some new *"business opportunity"* that will make me rich. When people call up with such enthusiasm about their new product and/or company and tell me how terrific it is, I listen. Of *course* it's the best. It's *their* chosen company—and chances are with this enthusiasm, they'll *make* it work. This doesn't mean, however, that this *company* is the best for you!

The first thing I need to know is *why* THEIR company is the best. Exactly how much *research* has this excited caller done on the background of the company? On its officers? On the product? How long has it been in business? What is their compensation plan? How many distributors does it have? Better yet, how much MONEY are these distributors making?

Chances are they know NONE of these answers. They attended a meeting and "heard"what the person in the front of the room told them and they liked what they heard and felt they could sell the product. And their *friend* who brought them to the meeting said it was okay.

## THE RIGHT PRODUCT

Without a doubt, the FIRST thing you look for is a company with a *unique* product or service that nobody else has. It could also be something that almost everyone NEEDS (or wants) that is CHEAPER and/or can be delivered *faster* than a competitive product. To appeal to the majority, that product or service must make them:

☆ **Feel better**
☆ **Look better**
☆ **Live longer**
☆ **Get things done quicker**
☆ **Enjoy life more**
☆ **Increase their gasoline mileage**
☆ **Save them money**
☆ **Make them money**

The product is vital. Think about it. If the product is the same as *everyone else is selling*, what are your odds? It's smart to choose a product the MAJORITY wants or needs. **Think** of any number of PRODUCTS, ones that work, that are safe and legal—that **you** would be inclined to buy and one that (hopefully)

NOBODY ELSE HAS!

## THE RIGHT COMPENSATION PLAN

On any job, one of the first few answers you need to get is, *How much money do I make? How do I get paid? When?* I'll spend much time talking about *money,* because that's the main topic in this book; how much MONEY can you earn in this business.

Again, everyone thinks *their* plan is best. The fact is, *most* Network Marketers *don't understand their own compensation plan* and couldn't explain it if their life depended upon it. They get involved in a company because a friend *sells* them on the program and too much of the time the friend doesn't understand what they are talking about either. People are *naive.* Many are just plain dumb.

They hear someone give a good speech, the person who brought them *to* the meeting (whether they've heard the speech a *thousand* times or more) will sit next to them and smile and laugh at tired jokes they've heard over and over that simply cannot *still* be funny, and they get their friend to sign a paper and join and *then* they discuss the compensation plan.

If you just want to *buy* whatever they are selling and want to get it *wholesale*, put the pencil to it, join if you can save money, get the stuff and try it. But if you plan on it bringing income, FIND OUT what you're going to make and UNDERSTAND how it works BEFORE you make any blind commitment. That's part of the RESEARCH I suggest you do. Here is what I recommend as far as the compensation plan:

I absolutely HATE a compensation plan that takes a college COURSE to understand. But if you find a product, you like the people, and the compensation plan IS complicated, have it explained to you *over and over* until you understand it.

If you are in Network Marketing, *somebody* in the organization will understand and be able to explain these plans to you. Enlist their help and listen to an explanation until you understand the plan *completely*. Remember, we're talking about money, and money counts. You have others who are depending on you so do NOT fail them by being gullible or lazy.

## THE RIGHT COMPANY

The company *must* have MONEY behind it. I do, however, know of several successful companies that began with a few people who pooled their credit cards and built a terrific organization. But for each one that succeeded, tens of thousands did not! Of ALL the companies that started on a shoestring, most ended up **hanging themselves with that same string.** *Research* the company as best you can

The next "ingredient" is the INTEGRITY and ABILITY of the company's CORPORATE OFFICERS. Without *qualified, experienced* leadership who have INTEGRITY, a company rarely becomes successful. You NEED corporate officers who KNOW what they're doing, who work hard and who are *good* people. Where can you find all of this? It's out there. You just have to look BEFORE you make a choice.

Talk with the officers and see if you get a *feeling*

about them. Find out from others what their background is in business and WHY they are qualified to RUN a business that YOU are going to spend time and money in. MOST of the time you can tell just being "around" these corporate officers. You don't have to LIKE them (of course that helps) but listen to them and try to determine what their qualities are that suit you.

## FOLLOW THE SYSTEM

If you join a new company, they have a SYSTEM to follow. No matter how hard or smart you work, the first rule of selling is that you KNOW what you're talking about. If not, how can you possibly tell others? You NEED to learn. Read the literature, listen to tapes, watch videos, attend meetings and training sessions and listen to what the one who sponsored you tells you. If you discover that they don't know what they're talking about or they neglect you, go to the one who sponsored *them*. You NEED proper training!

Too many want to work "their" way using "their" system. They want to "reinvent the wheel" and spend HOURS behind typewriters and computers writing and printing absolute JUNK, most of which is from amateurish, to awful, to downright embarrassing. They have NEVER been successful before in most things yet they will insist it be done THEIR way!

## GREEDY or STUPID

Yes, the **only** times I've lost on an investment was

when I was either greedy or stupid—or both. I either thought I could "make a killing" with little effort or didn't do my homework. When I am going to invest time and money in anything, the first thing I do is RESEARCH.

I would have to believe that the individual introducing me to this new Network Marketing company was an intelligent person with integrity. Also, I would have to like and want to use the product and see if I could afford (or want to take) the time required to become involved. Then, I'd set goals (surmountable ones). Remember, deal with this new venture as if it is—a business.

There's a saying, *"If you don't TAKE a chance, you never HAVE a chance!"* That one might not always apply in business UNLESS you have the time and money to lose. If you take that chance *without* research, it's a coin toss.

So, don't be sour on Network Marketing if it didn't work for you previously. It is still the *best chance* a "regular" person has to be financially independent, with very little money invested and virtually no previous experience or skills.

You will **always** run into people who just *do not believe* that Network Marketing works. Don't be offended by them, understand them and pray for them. *They just don't know that they don't know!*

Most are conservatives, or naive wage-earners who have no earthly conception of HOW Network Marketing really works. They could never, not in their wildest dreams, reason that *anyone* other than movie stars, CEO's of giant corporations, star athletes, or *dope dealers* could make 10, or 15 or 20 THOUSAND dollars a WEEK! These folks you can *never* convince. Don't try!

Can you imagine my telling them that I run into Network Marketers each WEEK who are earning $30,000 a MONTH during bad years? Thousands of them are driving luxury cars, living in mansions, and going on vacations for a *full month* only to return and find that they have more money in the bank than they had before they left! They are making RESIDUAL INCOME!

Think they'd believe that one of my friends was "stuck at" about $3,000 a month after 17 months in one Network Marketing company and within five months of using my new easy methods coupled with the age-old system, his check jumped to $36,000—a MONTH! And he wasn't one of the BIG money earners that used my methods.

The leaders in these many companies who worked smart and hard—who put in the hours and the time—are earning well over a MILLION dollars a year? If you told these non-believers that, they would swear that you were lying, crazy or stupid. But, it's true.

These non-believers are, mostly, the ones who never take a chance. They graduated from college, got a job, and that's all they know. They are either satisfied with their present job or won't tell you if they're not. Don't make fun of them, they're EVERYWHERE. No amount of convincing will alter their thinking, just pass them up. Do not LISTEN to them trying to dissuade you on taking a CHANCE, or deter you from giving yourself an OPPORTUNITY to change your life and lifestyle forever!

All most will do is tell you about that *"PYRAMID SCHEME business"* again. Let THEM keep working at a job they might hate. ABSENT yourself from negative and negative-thinking people. They are so negative they won't even listen to your side or read what ANY-ONE has to say about it. PASS THEM UP!

Egyptians built the true pyramids; they started at the bottom and built UP. With Network Marketing, you build like the Egyptians; start at the bottom and work up. And, *yes*, Network Marketing IS work. I never even implied that it was *easy* work, I only promised you the OPPORTUNITY to make a lot of money with no prior credentials, a small investment, and have a business of your own work. The amount you CAN earn is almost limitless.

**REMEMBER...
If it is to BE,
it is up to ME.**

## Chapter 3
## BEWARE

### I WAS AGAINST MLM

In 1980 I wrote a book on Multi-Level Marketing (former name for Network Marketing) and I *barbecued* the entire industry. The title was *The Truth About MLM,* with a skull and crossbones on the cover along with **BEWARE** in large letters followed by several giant exclamation marks.

Because, I had known and *known of* so many people who were led like sheep to the slaughterhouse into so many "get rich quick" deals involved with this type of selling. I warned of the pitfalls of MLM; the major ones no longer exist.

In that book, over 20 years ago, I listed what was necessary to have a SUCCESSFUL Multi-Level (Network Marketing) company and now, today, starting in the early 1990's there are many. You just have to know not only *what* to look for, but things to be wary *of.*

One large red flag (it's also ILLEGAL) is to *front load*—to have people *buy* their position by filling their garage full of products they can only *hope* to sell. Back then, many of the unknowing went bankrupt; they gave up their "regular" job and ended up losing their car, their HOUSE, their savings and sometimes, even their families.

So I went on an **ALL OUT CRUSADE** to stop these unfair businesses who hurt so many nice people. Yeah, I thoroughly BARBECUED the entire industry but, the government *changed the laws* and made it more *difficult* to get bilked by crooks in these type of businesses. Some of these "schemes", woefully, still exist and if you're **naive, gullible, greedy or stupid,** you'll go for them. Want a culprit? Don't blame the company. Look in the mirror.

But, if you deal from your HEAD and not from greed or stupidity, you have a chance. That's what I plan to give you; the best CHANCE there is to be successful in Network Marketing or ANY home-based business.

Never be SOLD on anything! EVERYBODY has the *best* plan, the *best* company, the *best* product, the best lawyer, doctor, dentist, tax accountant, spouse, etc., And THAT is one of the main ingredients in becoming *successful* in Network Marketing. You MUST believe in what you are marketing.

### STATISTICS

I'll not bombard you with *statistics*, because those aren't always accurate. It depends on *who* does the survey. Besides, I don't care what is happening in the financial world; my concern is what's going on in MY world—and YOURS!

I remember reading *statistics* when I was only a ten-year old. Statistics said, "*America was prosperous and that the average American family was earning*

*$10,000 a year."* You understand, this was a long time ago. My father was a house painter with a fourth grade education earning $35 a week BEFORE taxes and I don't want to add or multiply, but that was much less than **$10,000** a year. Guess we were below average.

When the roof leaked from 20 different places in the two-bedroom shack we lived in and we ran out of pots and pans to catch the water, we had to wait maybe three paydays to save the $7.50 for a roll of tar paper (included tar and nails). No, I didn't see **my** world as prosperous.

I'm not soliciting PITY when I tell you this. We didn't KNOW we were poor because EVERYBODY was poor. My father knew ONLY how to paint houses, and they never paid painters much. Certainly I loved him and I admired him, but as I grew older and a bit smarter, I knew that I never wanted to be poor and that it was up to only ME to change that.

As a fun-loving 21-year-old, there were more *statistics* that said, *"Ski Aspen! Guys, the women are* **eight deep** *at the bar."* I rushed to Aspen. This was one time statistics were correct; women WERE eight deep at the bar, but MEN were **TWENTY** deep! So much for statistics.

I don't care how the Network Marketing statistics are documented. Let's make them better. Let's talk about what can be done to help you—NOW!

### NO GUARANTEE

I use the word "CHANCE" often in this book because,

**THERE IS NO GUARANTEE!** Nor is there a guarantee in ANY business because there are a multitude of things that can go wrong. The biggest **guarantee** I can offer is YOU, your desire to make a lot of money, and the sacrifices YOU will have to make.

It makes me smile when people talk about "*get in the company early; get in on the ground floor.*" It is often smarter to get into MOST companies AFTER the first year since so many never make it to that 12-month test!

Too, during the first year there will ALWAYS be changes and glitches; it's impossible *not* to have them. There is absolutely NO WAY a company can predict how many distributors they will have in one month, two months, or six months.

It is *absolutely* impossible to store or produce or PREDICT how much PRODUCT you will sell at any given time, certainly not in the first year. And from the corporate standpoint, there will be people to hire, people to fire, people to promote, new methods of telecommunication, new products, and maybe a change in the marketing plan.

And, there is NO AMOUNT of advertising where EVERYBODY knows about your particular product, regardless of how unique it is. So "ground floor" or "getting in at the beginning" is a bunch of baloney.

I remember a product that I wrote a book about and the company boasted of over 200,000 distributors in two years. Many said "*they wish they had gotten in sooner.*" WHY? NOW was as good a time as any to get involved. The glitches are mostly out, the company has a much better idea on what to expect, they have chosen the best people, their pay plan is stabilized and they survived that first year! AND, there are over two hundred MILLION people in the US alone and most of them never heard of this product.

**There ARE no guarantees!** I remember when dozens of *Mom and Pop* shops in small towns were CLOSED because *Wal\*Mart* moved in. These people had been doing business and earning a living for generations! That's progress. These are changing times. This is LIFE! All the crying and moaning and complaining will do NO good. Start AGAIN! Try AGAIN! Lick your wounds and *"get back in the fight."*

The neighborhood bookstores are fast disappearing because these giant stores with a MILLION books come in and offer discounts, serve *Starbucks coffee,* and are great social gathering places. I love these big stores. This, also, is life.

Or some large company (not necessarily a *hostile takeover* situation) buys another large company and *management* changes. You might get a real *jerk* for a new boss, or you are laid off or forced into early retirement for "younger" and lesser salaried people.

No sir (ma'am), I want to be IN BUSINESS FOR MYSELF and Network Marketing is NOT "the wave of the future," it's here NOW! So, jump on the bandwagon, just make certain it's playing the music you like. Remember, ANYONE **CAN** DO IT! Some, of course, should NOT!

## JUMPERS

In every Network Marketing company there are those who do not do well, and go over to *another company* hoping to do better. Most *don't* do better! *"If they fail in San Francisco, chances are they'll fail in Tallahassee."* Were they lazy? Dumb? Chose the wrong product or company to represent? Didn't take time to learn? Or just are not "cut out" for dealing with people, or unable to work without being supervised?

With Network Marketing companies, you must work the SYSTEM! Oh, I'll give you ideas, ways, and options to *market* your products or *recruit* new people into your business, but the **system** is always what you must fall back on. WORK THE SYSTEM! Do not try to *reinvent* the wheel.

Network Marketing is WORK, hard work—and I can't emphasize that fact enough. Being RICH is hard work, too, and that's why I advocate working smart as well as hard. Smart is getting people to call **you**. Hard is going out to them; you must do *both* to prosper.

## BEST COMPANY—BEST PRODUCT

Every DAY I get at least two calls from people wanting me to join this company or that company and each of their companies is *the very best, and their PRODUCT is also the best!* You've been approached too, haven't you? Time and time again, right?

Because of my writing books on Network Marketing or Home-Based businesses, I have *"secret water from the Afghanistan,"* a machine that vibrates you like a snake (I love it!), the WRINKLE patch, some blue ointment that cures back pain instantly if I draw a line around to my navel or hip bones, I have finger and toe SPRINGS (love those too), and a glass triangle I'm supposed to chant over.

I have several breakfast malts for energy or weight loss, secret herbs from the Orient, BONES that I throw down to tell my fortune, a poem I recite while I allow myself to be enveloped in an imaginary golden BUBBLE that keeps away all negative thoughts, and a TON of vitamins in my garage that only the rats and roaches will become fat or healthy.

I have been sent ways to lower my taxes, to HIDE my money in some group of islands or archipelago in the Caribbean, to INVEST my money wisely by sending CASH out to a post office box (Pyramid Scheme), and an elixir that grows hair on bald heads. Then there's *another* that I found fascinating; a salve that makes the BREAST larger but ONLY if you rub the *gizzum* on COUNTER clockwise! **BeWARE! Be WARY. Be CAREFUL. Be SMART.**

The tax people are superb, SOME of the breakfast malts I drink, and some of the vitamins I take. The WRINKLE patch works, but you must continue it for life. The finger and toe springs actually DO relax me and the "golden bubble" idea works too. The "snake" machine oxygenizes my blood and keeps my back aligned and also helps me sleep, and that pre-paid legal plan is superb.

There is also a company that brought 40 years of RESEARCH done by the Russians on their athletes, their military, their Cosmonauts and their elite, to this country. Athletes in the 1994 Atlanta Olympics used this product and 187 or the 192 who DID use it won medals. I have that and I take it daily. There are SEVERAL excellent NEW products "out there" and you just have to find them.

NOW, that BREAST ENLARGER CREAM "sounded" good to me until it was explained that if it was rubbed CLOCKWISE on breasts, it would make them SMALLER (or *vice versa*). I suggest you READ THE DIRECTIONS CAREFULLY before attempting to use this. And MEN, if you assist your wife, be careful if you SCRATCH soon afterward! Make certain it's CLOCKWISE—or is it COUNTER clockwise?

Yes, I get at least a dozen calls each week from people who want to interest me in joining or writing a book about their product. If it's a friend, I listen for TWO minutes and if it's something I haven't heard of before, I ask that they mail or e-mail the information. I won't even accept a FAX anymore because EVERY plan I've been sent is longer than the *Dead Sea Scrolls* and I run out of fax paper. But, I DO listen for those two minutes because it just MIGHT be some-thing new and exciting. In making a selection to work for a company and/or with their product, I ask that you work from the **head** and choose wisely.

Network Marketing is no different than any other business—EXCEPT—you can make *more money* in it with such a *small investment.* And, really, anyone CAN do it but some should not even try.

## THOSE WHO SHOULD NOT DO IT

If you are NOT organized.
If you DON'T like people.
If you are SATISFIED with your job and income.
If you have NO extra time to try.
If you are *convinced* it's a Pyramid Scheme.
If you'd rather spend free time watching TV.


There must be a few more reasons but, at the moment, I can't think of any.


**MONEY, does not buy happiness.
BUT, it certainly makes MISERY
easy to endure**

## Chapter 4
# WINNERS

Many "in the business" say you must have a *consumable* to be successful: NOT necessarily so! *Excel* sells telephones; *Alpine (EcoQuest)* markets air purifiers; *Nikken* sells MAGNETS; *Pre-Paid Legal* sells services. ALL are excellent, successful companies. There's auto care, dental care, insurance, kitchen ware, and water filters. A good company has good management, an excellent *proven* product, and a pay plan that is "distributor friendly." GO with the unique product and a reputable company, and you won't make an error.

This list of companies on the following page is BY NO MEANS up to date, but it gives you an IDEA on some of the different companies and products, and all I can really GUARANTEE is that they began their businesses in the year mentioned.

The number of distributors they STATE doesn't mean it's fact, and there are several new companies since then who are doing well. Too, the number of distributors fluctuates and some companies tell an outright LIE to work themselves higher up the ladder.

| RANK | # OF DIST. | COMPANY NAME / PRODUCT LINE | START DATE |
|------|-----------|-----------------------------|------------|
| 1 | 4,000,000 | Forever Living / Nutritionals, etc. | 1978 |
| 2 | 2,500,000 | Amway / Home Care, etc. | 1959 |
| 3 | 750,000 | Herbalife / Nutritionals, etc. | 1980 |
| 4 | 620,000 | Excel / Telephone | 1988 |
| 5 | 500,000 | Sunrider / Nutritionals, etc. | 1982 |
| 6 | 500,000 | Mary Kay / Cosmetics | 1963 |
| 7 | 500,000 | Neways / Nutritionals, etc. | 1986 |
| 8 | 450,000 | Life Plus / Nutritionals, etc. | 1970 |
| 9 | 445,000 | Avon / Cosmetics | 1886 |
| 10 | 400,000 | Shaklee / Nutritionals, etc. | 1956 |
| 11 | 385,000 | Nature's Sunshine / Nutritionals, etc. | 1974 |
| 12 | 300,000 | Essentially Yours Industries / Nutritionals, etc. | 1996 |
| 13 | 220,000 | Cell Tech / Nutritionals, etc. | 1991 |
| 14 | 220,000 | Rexall / Nutritionals, etc. | 1990 |
| 15 | 200,000 | NSA / Nutritionals, etc. | 1970 |
| 16 | 152,000 | Enviro-Tech / Auto Care, etc. | 1991 |
| 17 | 150,000 | Melaleuca / Nutritionals, etc. | 1985 |
| 18 | 150,000 | Enrich / Nutritionals, etc. | 1986 |
| 19 | 135,000 | Alpine (now EcoQuest) Air Purifiers | 1989 |
| 20 | 100,000 | Nikken / Magnets, etc. | 1989 |
| 21 | 100,000 | Nu Skin / Skin Care | 1984 |
| 22 | 100,000 | Nutrition For Life / Nutritionals, etc. | 1984 |
| 23 | 100,000 | Oxyfresh / Dental Care | 1984 |
| 24 | 100,000 | Primerica / Insurance | 1977 |
| 25 | 100,000 | Tupperware / Kitchenware | 1951 |
| 26 | 100,000 | Equinox / Air & Water Filters | 1991 |

Other seemingly successful companies with less than 100,000 distributors (maybe MORE by now) are—**Achievers, Matol, Body Wise, F.I.N.L., IDN, Reliv, Usana, Watkins, Jafra, Nanci, Viva America, Royal Body Care, Market America, Life Science Technologies, First Fitness, and Fuller Brush.**

The source for this chart is the combined result of information from our contacts with the individual companies, *Wealth Building Magazine, Money Maker's Monthly* and the *Direct Selling Association.*

Do not misconstrue this list as an endorsement or recommendation of any kind, it's meant only to convey my knowledge of their existence. Go with the company and product you feel most comfortable with, and the people you enjoy being around.

The NUMBER of distributors for each of these companies is in constant flux. It is NOT an indication of how well a company is doing. I've seen companies boast of 300,000 or 500,000 distributors and they get greedy and change the marketing plan, up the price on their products, change their product line, the president leaves with the money, or they make some stupid error and the company is OVER or they lose many of their distributors.!

What I want to know about a company is not how MANY distributors they list, but . . .

✔ **How many CHECKS they pay out each month.**
✔ **What is the total pay out.**
✔ **How long they've been in business.**
✔ **How many of their *original distributors* they have since their first few years in the business**
✔ **What PERCENTAGE of their distributors are making "reasonable"money ($50,000 a year or more)**

*These* are the statistics that never lie!

Find OUT about these companies, talk to people who have been IN these companies for months or years and LOOK AT their checks. Do not listen to that "silk suit" in the front of the room who tells you how EASY it is, because it is NOT easy! It's darn hard. It just happens to be the EASIEST and the FASTEST avenue for you to be able to get RICH. I've seen it happen too many times.

At ALL of these meetings (if they are handled correctly) you will get people out of the audience who give their personal TESTIMONIES. The "new rules" don't allow folks to talk about MONEY, but MONEY is the reason most people are there. When I'M giving a speech or seminar on a home-based business, I certainly talk about money.

And don't be deceived by the way a person LOOKS when they give these testimonials. Often, one person in the audience looks at the person next to them and says, "*If HE (or she) did it, I know that I can.*" Seems right but not necessarily so. GUTS, DESIRE, WORK ETHICS, PERSEVERANCE are NOT evident on the way they look, talk, dress or "come across." And, like many of you, I thought that, too. I've been guilty of both saying and thinking it.

As I mentioned earlier, the ONLY ones I'd advise NOT to try Network Marketing are those who *love* their jobs, are *satisfied* with their lifestyle, and have no TIME, because TIME is what you need to build a business and TIME is what makes the business build FOR you once you learn "the system"and learn to DUPLICATE.

Earning a SALARY at a JOB is what is called "linear" income; you only make more if you work faster or put in longer hours. In Network Marketing, you get what is termed "residual" income; you make money even when you DON'T work. That is, if you worked the SYSTEM and you DUPLICATED yourself; you trained others to do as you have done and you build and build and BUILD.

SOME have made a lot of money in Network marketing by finding a product that was UNIQUE and they were able to RETAIL the product. And that's fine, BUT, it's almost the same as a JOB and that "linear" income term kicks in again. When YOU stop advertising, when YOU stop retailing, when YOU stop putting in the hours and the effort, your income comes to a sliding halt! I suggest you do both; sell AND duplicate.

The word NETWORK means you tell others about whatever it is you're selling. MARKETING means that you have found ways to MOVE your product! What SMARTER way is there than to get other "hole diggers" to help, and you, personally, PAY THEM NOTHING? When you TEACH them to dig those holes, when you DUPLICATE your own efforts, you are working SMART and you are producing "residual" income; when you sleep, or rest, or vacation and they are still digging, YOU are making money and THEY are making money. As they get more diggers to help, then THEY, also, are receiving *residual* income.

Perhaps digging holes is a bad example because somewhere *down the line* you run out of money to pay the diggers, right? WRONG! As you grow and grow to vast proportions, you can't expect to make a dollar a hole of 50 cents per hole, but like that golf game, if you get but PENNIES from diggers or a SINGLE penny and you have thousands, tens of thousands and HUNDREDS of thousands of people digging ditches, you are **NOW—ENORMOUSLY WEALTHY!**

It's the way Network Marketing works, folks. It is EASY to understand, and it is EASIER to make **big money** in Network Marketing than any other (legal) way I know. I see it happening every day with the most unlikely *looking* people. And, if THEY can do it, so can you. **You CANNOT get rich working a JOB, or working for someone else!**

If I went busted tomorrow morning, by noon I would be in a Network Marketing company and in my own home-based business.

## HOW TO CHOOSE A WINNING COMPANY

Truthfully, it's like choosing a spouse; 50% fail the FIRST time, another 50% fail the SECOND time, but if you learn to choose *academically* as well as from the heart your odds increase. And if YOU are willing to make some changes, some concessions, to sacrifice some of your free time and TRY, you'll have a chance. There are some prerequisites to being in business for yourself, and if you understand your own strong and weak points, that's a good way to start.

If you, personally, are not **100% committed** to *whatever* you're doing, chances are it won't work. If you need help, GET help from your spouse or close friend. I personally, am about 75% PERFECT for some things, but that's not enough. It's like a relay race with four runners; if three or those runners are fast, and one is a *clog,* you will NEVER win the race. If you plan to earn BIG money, find someone who is maybe 75% also, but *their* seventy-five covers your missing twenty-five.

Let's take these attributes one at a time and if YOU don't have them all, find that partner, that back-up person you can count on and work together.

### ORGANIZE

One of the basic rules for being in business for yourself is TIME MANAGEMENT. Your *time* is your income; try to spend it wisely. No matter how *hard* you work, how *smart* you work, or what you accomplish, you need to **keep records** and this requires doing. . .

### PAPERWORK

Regardless of the *number* of people you recruit and sponsor, or how much *product* you sell, it must be properly RECORDED on paper. Make certain you know **exactly** how to do it or all of your efforts will be lost. Ask your SPONSOR to teach and assist you with all of it until you are convinced that you know the correct procedure.

This paperwork is as important as a will. If it's filled out incorrectly, the person you like LEAST might get all of your money. So, get help. If you are not the type who can keep things in order, enlist help from your spouse, mother, sponsor or somebody. Who knows? You might even recruit your helper to become active in your *downline*. After you learn to correctly fill out the paperwork, you need to keep track of your progress; you need to fully understand about . . .

## VOLUME

How much VOLUME do you have? *People* certainly count, but GOOD people count more. I've seen some *lucky* Network Marketers who enrolled only five or ten people and they are making hundreds of thousands of dollars per year. Then, I've seen some who had *thousands* of people and they were making school-teacher's pay. It isn't "warm bodies" or names, it's the VOLUME of sales that count.

## PROSPECTING

Identifying people to recruit for your downline is called PROSPECTING. Just for the heck of it, make a list of EVERYONE YOU KNOW. You'll be surprised to find that you will end up with several *hundred* names—or more. If the Network Marketing company you choose is on the ball, they'll include a sample list in your marketing kit. If not, try this:

When you get up tomorrow morning, have a legal pad and pencil close by to carry with you. If your first move is toward the bathroom, think about talking to your plumber, the salesperson when you go replace your toilet seat, or the people in the grocery where you buy your toilet paper.

When you open your medicine cabinet to get tooth paste, think about talking to your dentist, their assistant, the receptionist. Look at the pills in that cabinet; talk to your doctor, his receptionist, his nurse, people in the waiting room and your pharmacist.

As you put your clothes on, think about talking to the person who sells you pants, a skirt, underwear, shoes. Lost weight? *Gained* weight? How about your seamstress or tailor?

The telephone is ringing. Tell WHOEVER IT IS about your new business. Talk to the telephone repair person, the billing clerk, the person who sells you an additional telephone.

Is it too cold or too warm? Write down the name of your air-conditioning repair person, the meter reader, the secretary at the main office. And on, and on, and on.

I won't walk you to the kitchen or throughout your entire *day*, I just wanted you to start THINKING. You know, know *of*, or meet hundreds of people. You pass them, greet them, or visit with them each day. I want you to realize how LIMITLESS your potential is and how endless your list of prospects are.

At work, talk with everyone. At lunch, talk to the waitress. On the way home and passing a toll booth on the expressway, hand the person in that little house a brochure with your name and number on it.

Talk with the mail carrier, clerks at the post office, leave a brochure with them. Get your grass cut?

House cleaned? Get the house painted? Speak with them and offer your brochure. Go to the bank? Hand the teller a brochure. Get some plants or garden soil? Leave them a brochure. You get the idea.

You are now in the PEOPLE business, and the more people you talk to the better your CHANCES of being successful in Network Marketing. The ONLY limitation you have is your own desire and effort to make it work.

### THE THREE-FOOT RULE

This means that when anyone comes within *three feet* of wherever you are, you tell them about what you're marketing. Well, it works for some and *scares the daylights* out of others. If you want to give yourself the best odds at being successful in Network Marketing, do it. It works. Most of the successful Network Marketers *swear* by it. At least try it.

Look around you. There are truly nice people in the world. If you have a brochure, stick it in their hand as you pass by. They won't hit you or cuss at you. They might even *call* you if your brochure interests them. The very worst that will happen is that they'll toss it on the ground. Then, somebody else might pick it up and call. EFFORT pays off.

### FOLLOW UP

Whew! But is THIS important! After your initial call or contact with a person, call them within a few days and

FOLLOW UP! If you don't follow up, you fail. It's that simple. Ask them if they'd like to know more. If they say *yes,* invite them to a meeting or go meet with them at their convenience or send information to them. They NEED to know that you are interested enough in what you're doing to find out how they are doing, so FOLLOW UP.

It is a known fact among professional sales people that very few sales are made from an *initial contact* alone. If you ask the top salesperson in any field, "What is your **best** sales technique?" They will reply with two words, "FOLLOW UP!"

### RECRUIT and SPONSOR

Recruit only, **and you'll fail**. *Of COURSE* you must recruit to get people, just add *sponsor* to that. Recruit AND Sponsor and you'll win. Here's the difference.

When you *recruit* a person, you just sign them up. *Marines* recruit! They talk to some kid fresh out of high school and tell them all the wondrous things about being a Marine. Those "recruiters" are dressed in their pressed uniforms with all sorts of medals pinned over their left breast pocket. They are just that: Marine **RECRUITERS**. They do what "recruiters" do; "enroll" the kids, turn them loose, forget about them, and they never see the kids again.

But to SPONSOR someone is different. When you *sponsor,* you become *responsible* for that person. TEACH them the business. Teach them how to teach. Show them the best way to become successful. You

SHOW THEM how to go out and sponsor others. Do a good job for them and they'll do one for you.

To do it correctly, help them set an appointment with someone close to them. YOU go along *with* them. YOU do the talking because YOU are their sponsor, their mentor, and YOU know the business. Help them until they get it right.

What you're doing now is TRAINING. You teach that person what **duplication** is. You are building your business by showing them how Network Marketing works. Once they are trained properly and really see it in action, they will go out and do the same thing.

With several of these people in your *downline* (you are their *upline*) you are DOUBLING your own efforts, then redoubling them. You are starting with a PENNY bet on 18 holes and by *training others,* by **duplication**, you will be earning that big money.

## MARKETING

Since this is the only way to move your product or service, getting "the word" out to people is necessary. The question is, HOW to do it in the least expensive way and get the best results? Below is a fun example of smart marketing.

About 50 years ago in Louisiana, there was a man named Dudley LeBlanc who began a magnificent marketing campaign for his product called *Hadacol.* I don't even think *Amway* was around then.

He sent over a dozen telephone solicitors into Atlanta, New Orleans, Dallas and Houston. These are supposedly the most difficult southern cities to sell anything new. Each worker was told to sit in their hotel room and call the various pharmacies and grocery stores (before supermarkets even) and ask if they had *Hadacol* in stock. The question always came back; "What's *Hadacol?*" And they were told, not sold.

After a week of making hundreds of calls a day each, they changed cities and began the calling again. The calls went on for a solid month. Then, in comes a band playing *The Hadacol Boogie* followed by dozens of trucks loaded down with *Hadacol.*

The merchants rushed to get their *allotted* cases of *Hadacol.* Some paid extra *under the table money* to truck drivers to get double and triple the amount LeBlanc set for them. These store owners WANTED the *Hadacol* because they were convinced that their customers wanted it.

I even remember a verse or two of their song.

> *"The rooster and the hen were sittin' in the shade.*
> *The hen did the boogie while the rooster layed the egg.*
> *He did the Hadacol Boogie, the Hadacol Boogie, the Hadacol Boogie makes you Boogie Woogie all the time."*

The store owners lined their shelves with lots of *Hadacol* and put up huge signs. When the customers saw this humongous display, they bought *Hadacol.*

Everybody loved *Hadacol;* it was said to have cured a multitude of ills. Later it was discovered that it was 33% alcohol. No WONDER it made people feel good; if they drank enough, they all became intoxicated!

I'm not certain of the accuracy of the *Hadacol* scenario, whether my dad told me what was true or what he believed to be true, but I remember that song. (If we meet, ask me to sing a verse for you). So, whether or not this is exactly how it happened is irrelevant; that's MARKETING.

Another example of marketing I recall hearing about was when the first sardines were introduced to Americans. A company canned PINK sardines. The problem was, pink sardines were very rare whereas WHITE sardines were plentiful.

The public's demand for these pink sardines was so great that the fishermen couldn't catch enough of the smelly little things. A new company emerged and tried to sell WHITE sardines. Consumers wouldn't buy them; they wanted the PINK delicacies.

That's when some marketing genius wrote a powerful message using only eight words on the can of the white sardines:

---

## GUARANTEED NOT
## TO TURN PINK
## IN THE CAN

---

Smart marketing, huh?

## Chapter 5
# MEETINGS AND MONEY

I know, you *hate* going to meetings and you have tried and *tried* to get your friends to go to at least one meeting and it is next to impossible. I, personally, *love* meetings because I like people. And meetings, like them or not, are the LIFEBLOOD of every Network Marketing company. If you don't enjoy meetings, **learn** to enjoy them because they are the very best way to increase your business. Period.

You LEARN at meetings, and learning is what is foremost in this business. You learn from the person conducting the meeting and you learn from others present at the meeting. Then you begin trying to get your friends and prospects to a meeting.

## GETTING FRIENDS TO MEETINGS

Most people hate being SOLD anything. Also, most people have been to a meeting involving selling something and they will use *every excuse* in the world NOT to go with you. The second you tell them it's an "opportunity" meeting, an *invisible wall* appears that even *Superman* can't break through. Most have heard of an "opportunity" meeting and they don't want an *opportunity,* so PLEASE don't call it that.

People LIE to **not** go to an "opportunity meeting" even with their best friend. They just *know* you're going to try to get them to sell make-up, soap, vitamins, floor polish, invest in a bank in the Cayman Islands, or go in with them in a timeshare condo with 50 others for your one-week-per-year vacation in Bosnia. If they've lived long enough, chances are they have been very disappointed by one company or another and they want no part of any MEETING.

Even if they (finally) agree to have you pick them up at their home, there have been instances where the ENTIRE FAMILY turns out all the lights and lies *face down on the floor* afraid to breathe, with hopes that you stop ringing their doorbell or pounding on their door. They'll make up a good lie for you in the morning once they've had time to think about it.

More friendships have been broken by a person in Network Marketing who uses the WRONG approach to get friends to a meeting than anything in the world (other than relatives acting as bone-pickers when a will is read).

So, find the *best way you can think of* to invite a friend to a meeting. But, please *don't deceive* them pretending you're inviting them out to eat or to a movie. I've found that the best approach is to ask them to accompany you to the meeting as a personal favor to you as you'd rather not go alone.

If you take but ONE NEW PERSON a week to a meeting for one year, your chances of becoming successful in Network Marketing is almost guaranteed. You have put the odds in your favor.

When you bring a guest, even if you've heard

the same presentation a *thousand* times, still *look* as interested as if it were your first time. If you get up, or move around, or become seemingly bored, so will your guest. Remember this is the FIRST DATE. Be at your very best and it will increase the odds of your guest responding favorably.

If your guest is interested in making money, keep them there *after* the main meeting and explain the compensation plan. I'd NEVER recommend you talk money unless your guest is really interested. First, talk PRODUCT, friendships, and fun. Most people can use a few new friends and everybody likes fun.

If you invite (or take) your new guest to a FUN meeting, that guest will bring a new guest with them the *following* week. This is a great method to create your *downline* organization and build your business.

Getting a new person to a meeting every week is the tough part. Persistence pays off. Work on several people each week to improve your odds. I would choose the approach that fits your personality.

Here are a few ideas: (You, to your friend) *"I just learned of a terrific new company that I'm considering being a part of. I value your opinion and I want you to hear what they say and have you advise me."* (This approach has been used often, but it still works.)

Let's say you just delivered the above "opinion pitch" to a friend. If they've been an adult for five or so years, chances are they've heard it before. Typical reply:

(Your friend's reply) *"If this is one of those stupid **pyramid** deals, don't do this to me. Don't drag me in with you."* (This is where you "sort of" level with him.)

(You) *"I'm already IN it. (No need to lie, he's on to you) and I really and truly LIKE it. You're my friend. I've gone several places with you that I didn't want to go, so all I'm asking is that you tell me what you think."* (Press a little. You believe in what you're doing.)

It's no big deal to call in a *marker.* If you've been friends long enough, you each owe the other for a bad date, bad vacation, bad meal, bad movie, bad *something.* Be truthful. But, be creative and find a way to drag them to that meeting. You're clever and innovative, think of a way. Straightforward honesty, I've found, is the best method for everything.

If it's an acquaintance, tell them about the product and/or the compensation plan, invite them to dinner or drink before the meeting. Agree to pick them up to (almost) assure that they will be at the meeting.

If it's a friend, relative or a loved one, you *owe* it to them to share your good fortune, to help them find something that might change their lives for the better. If you **believe** in what you're doing, so will they. Do NOT badger them; even if they join they are not worth the trouble to constantly convince or motivate them.

## GOOD MEETINGS vs BAD MEETINGS

ONE "bad"meeting runs off prospects—that *night.* A few bad meetings in a *row,* and you *might* be out of business! Meetings should not last longer than ONE HOUR, maybe a *little* longer, UNLESS, you're having fun and so is everyone else. If you want to stay longer, there will always be little "bunches" of people at a table or in the corner of the room talking. Ease on over and listen, you might learn something interesting.

If that person conducting the meeting cannot drive their PRODUCT INFORMATION across in 60 minutes or so, find another meeting. If you have a guest who wants to *learn about the product*, do not take them to a meeting where they will be *sold* or *brainwashed* on a compensation plan.

Often, on bad meetings, the person conducting the meeting either *reads* information (BIG mistake), or becomes so enamored with their own voice that they lull you to sleep.

Meetings should start ON TIME! They have to be both informative *and* fun. If you're new in the business, have your sponsor, mentor, or favorite *upline* help you with that person you bring to the meeting. But again, only to *inform*, not sell.

Sing the praises of both the product and the company. Introduce your guest to some people you know and like. Make them feel important and smile a lot. If the meeting coordinator is not to your liking, or has a reputation of being too long and is boring, **DO NOT WASTE A PROSPECT BY TAKING THEM THERE!** Tell them about the plan yourself or get your mentor to do it.

How am I such an authority on meetings? I've been a guest speaker at least 5,000 times at both good and bad meetings; I know a good one from a bad one. I've given both.

## HOME MEETINGS

What if you are *first* in your area and there are *no* meetings? Begin with a home meeting. Invite friends and neighbors and family to a "gathering" at your home. Don't know much? *Learn!* Remember, if you don't know what you're talking about, how can you explain it to others?

When you learn what you're talking about, have that home meeting of six or eight or how many you can comfortably seat, and share your enthusiasm and knowledge with them. It has to begin somewhere, and home meetings can be easier to get people to attend. They're your friends, they can easily walk or drive to your home. If you're new in the business, have your *sponsor* conduct the meeting.

Whether you serve refreshments, cookies or snacks is up to you. Try to have the kids out of the house, and either put your telephone on an answer machine (first ring) or pull out the plug. You need to be able to focus your attention on your subject as you speak. *And*, you need *their* UNDIVIDED attention.

## REGIONAL MEETINGS and CONVENTIONS

I LIKE both. Network Marketing companies have regional meetings to make certain that any bad *local* meetings are buffered by professional ones. Take your new prospects to *these* meetings. This is part of the company's support system to help their distributors.

Conventions are the **best** meetings to attend. If

you can entice a person you want to sponsor to a *convention*, they WILL be impressed. The speakers are usually chosen for their ability to communicate and they are usually the *elite* of the company. They are the ones who know how to *make things happen*. You can learn from them.

ALL companies "honor" their top income producers, but this doesn't qualify that top earner **to speak**; I say give them cash bonuses, trips, or new cars but if they are NOT good speakers, pat them on the back, give them their award, let them WAVE at the audience and—SIT THEM DOWN! Do NOT let them say ANYTHING! Let ONLY the ones who speak well, **speak!**

## MY IDEAS ON A MEETING

Distributors are what makes it possible for a Network Marketing company to stay in business; the more distributors, the more products are sold.

My feelings are, if a company has a PRODUCT that is outstanding, they should focus on the PRODUCT. And if they DON'T have an outstanding product, they shouldn't be in business. The PRODUCT sells and IS the business! You NEED distributors for the product, and what better way to GET distributors to SELL that product than have them 100% committed TO that product. When THEY believe, they are set to go out and convince others.

MANY who are involved in these Network marketing companies are in them to HELP OTHERS first and the money is secondary. In THIS book, I'm talking only about MONEY, but what BETTER way is there to MAKE money than by helping others feel good, live longer, become happier AND make money?

I have another friend, a delightful, fun, warm, caring ALIEN—(let's call him TIM, since that's his name) who has a TERRIFIC product which he believes in wholeheartedly, and he also CARES about helping others—to FEEL better AND to make MONEY.

At HIS meetings, he goes RIGHT for them joining the business and THEN talks about the product afterward. HE is successful using this approach, and I applaud him, but very few OTHERS can do *his* way.

MY method is to focus on PRODUCT. Don't let the audience SEE the product; HIDE it under a tablecloth to one side, and when the meeting is OVER, have a GRAND UNVEILING. I want the audience to listen to what I have to SAY about the product and not be looking at the bottles or boxes or items thinking, *"How much is THAT going to cost me?"*

NO! I want them to focus on the SPEAKER, and then AFTER the speech I'd say something like...
*"Now, let's SEE the product I've been talking about and HOW MUCH each it costs."*

THEN, I'd *whip* that cloth back like the unveiling of a statue, and hold up a FEW of the items (use your LEAD items only, the others they can find out about from the person who brought them to the meeting) and as I tell the price. THIS is when I tell them about the business. I sort of "slip in" on them, NEVER deceiving them or pushing them.
*"Now, you've heard the price. How many*

*would like to buy the product WHOLESALE?"*
(Almost ALL hands go up, right? Who DOESN'T want
*wholesale?* This is when I get right down to it.

*"Folks, you were brought here tonight by a
friend who wanted you to advise them on, or join
them in a business. You've seen the product(s),
you know the price, and if you want it wholesale,
it's simple, you just buy several bottles (or whatever) and enjoy a QUANTITY discount!*

*"NOW, I'd like to find out how many would
like to get the product FREE?"* (ALL hands *certainly*
go up here, but they know there's a catch so, without
wasting time or TRYING to deceive them, I say...)

*"For those of you who want to buy one or
two bottles* (or whatever you're selling) *or want it
wholesale and purchase several bottles, I'm going
to have about a 15-minute break so you can do
that. BEFORE you get up, we will have ANOTHER
short session maybe 15 minutes at the most, to
tell you how you CAN get it FREE and even make
some money with it."*

LET those who only want to TRY the product,
get their product and LEAVE. If they WANT to learn
how to get it FREE, and if you've given a good meeting, they will STAY for WHATEVER you have to tell
them. You said "*only 15- minutes,*" so MAKE it only 15
minutes and let the one who brought them tell them
more.

MY thoughts are that IF the product is what you
say it is, you'll GET these people BACK and they will
be WILLING to listen to WHATEVER it is you have to

say. The ones who stay for your extra 15-minute talk are the ones who ARE interested in getting it FREE or in making money distributing it.

This, of course, is MY way of conducting a meeting. Find the best way for YOU, and do it. There are several TYPES of meetings, and if the audience KNOWS they are there to learn about a BUSINESS, go right at them. If not, EXPLAIN your product and let THEM come back to YOU. When they do, they are ready to be trained and you are ready to DUPLICATE yourself.

If the COMPANY insists that you do your meetings THEIR way, *do it their way* because they know better than you and better than I (sounds better if I say "better than ME!" But, I think "I" is correct.

NEVER *bug or badger* friend or relative to join; they do it just to get you *off their butt*. You'll only waste a LOT of TIME trying to *get* them to work. If friends and relatives don't BELIEVE in Network Marketing, hand them this book, give them 5 days to read it and then PICK UP THE BOOK! If they join, fine. And if not, get the book back and give it to someone else! The BOOK sells them and if not, they truly are NOT prospects.

Using MY methods takes the **SELLING** out, and the **TELLING** in. You need not **EVER** have to **SELL** anyone on what you're doing. NEW people in this business will know that what I'm saying makes sense, and the "experienced" ones will recognize it as a Godsend. My methods CHANGE it all, and make it such that . . .

*Chapter 6*
# WORKING SMART

Yes, I think the OLD way—*alone*—is tough to work and the reason why so many do not even *attempt* Network Marketing. *I'd rather "run naked through saw grass"* than continuously try to SELL people.

You see, the word *"marketing"* means *"selling,"* and many people don't want to, don't know *how* to, or just *can't* SELL! Certain personalities are just not conducive to selling *anything*. So, MY methods are new—and they WORK!

## MY METHODS

I have devised several ways to get people (mostly STRANGERS) coming to **YOU**, asking **YOU**, calling **YOU** to find out about how THEY can get involved in either BUYING something that you happen to have, or JOINING whatever it is you are in; you don't SELL, you simply TELL them about it.

By using these methods, all you need to do is LEARN what you're going to TELL them about. It puts *Network Marketing* in a new light. It opens the door for many who shied away from it in the past. It's SMART marketing and all you need to do is WANT to be in business for yourself and be able to talk—to just answer questions.

If YOU want to make money in this business, let me tell you how you can use ME to do it! For instance, most people feel an *author* is someone who is bright. And most people *think* that being an author is something special, and that authors are rich! The fact is, *most* authors make little or NO money, and some would STARVE if they didn't have other jobs.

Years ago I recall reading in one newspaper or other that of the 500 *lowest* paying jobs, number 500 was a *migrant farm worker,* and number 499 was a *freelance author*! I'M freelance, but I found a "system" and I FOLLOW that system.

I write books on TOPICS that appeal to the *majority*. I find a good title, attractive cover, write in BIG print, words that you don't need a college degree or a dictionary to read, I research them with the tenacity of a PIT BULL, I tell you the TRUTH, I make my books less than 100 pages (since most people either HAVE no time, or TAKE no time, or maybe have a short attention span), and the books sell for less than ten dollars. THIS book is a perfect example.

## USE THIS BOOK

Other than the information you get from *reading* this book, you can start *selling* it, *giving* it away, or using it as an *incentive* for people to buy your particular product—*whatever* it is.

Simply GET IT TO as many people as you can whom you feel would like to be in business for themselves. Let IT sell them on the business; let it TELL them what this business is all about.

If, after reading this book, they don't call you for more information, they are either already rich, or they are not prospects. Once they read about Network Marketing, they will learn that they have a CHANCE to change their financial life FOREVER. Now, let me tell you how I am willing to help you, and . . . it's **FREE!**

### RADIO SHOWS

There are *thousands* of talk shows being aired each day with hosts who *hunger* for new material. They oftentimes need upwards of 1,000 topics per year if they have a one-hour show, and they LIKE controversial subjects, Network Marketing IS a subject most can relate to and many will listen to.

I have been on the radio at least 1,000 times in the past four months talking about how people get rich by networking. The results are that an average of 112 people per broadcast call YOU to find out WHAT IT IS YOU'RE DOING. And, you TELL them. The BOOK **sells** them on the theory, YOU tell them about your product or service! It's from difficult to impossible to get even *friends and relatives* to attend a meeting. So, work on *strangers*; they're easier to talk to anyway, especially if they ask YOU!

These talk shows (that are EVERYWHERE) have hosts and program directors who HUNT for new material daily. A book on starting up your own home-based business is certainly *evocative* because SO

MANY people want to make big money and start a business of their own.

I tell them WHY they failed before and how they can make it THIS time. Radio hosts LOVE to interview an author, and HOME-BASED BUSINESSES is one terrific topic. And MOST who have FAILED want to LEARN how to make it. The ones who say, "It's a *Pyramid Scheme* will get an education.

I'LL help FREE—IF you want to work, IF you want to change your FINANCIAL LIFE, IF you are willing to put in the time. If not, please do NOT call! My "mission" is to help. The cost is ZERO. It's the fastest way I'VE found to get YOUR product advertised FREE. All YOU have to do is stay at home, and answer the calls, and TELL the caller about it. You have them In YOUR backyard, on YOUR turf, in YOUR arena.

## I'LL DO MEETINGS FOR YOU

Call me, plug me in to YOUR MEETING, and I'll give 8 or 10 or 15 minutes of information to YOUR group that you gathered from the radio show on the wonders *of,* and the opportunity *with,* Network Marketing.

Do you see, I'M doing part of the meeting FOR you. It gives you time to observe the new faces in the crowd, their reactions to what I say, and make your plan on how to interest them on what you're doing.

HOW can I do this for EVERYONE? I can't! You see, MOST will not ask my help; some are lazy, some will quit, some won't TRY, some are stupid, and some use their "old" methods (that failed before), and some will try to "reinvent the wheel". YOU choose.

## TALK TO GROUPS

The SECOND best way to interest people in what you're marketing is for YOU to speak to groups. If ONE person in that group "goes for" whatever you are marketing, chances are you'll get the *entire group*. Plus, you're "pitching" the *program director* when you tell them about a home-based business and perhaps THEY are interested in trying. If YOU can't do these meetings, find someone in your organization who can.

If you want a new, *warm* market of total strangers, contact *longevitymedia.com (my service company)* on your computer or call my office for the free packet of information. It's MY gift to YOU for buying and reading this book. Call ONLY if you're serious about wanting to start your own home-based business. It COULD change your life.

## Chapter 7
## LISTEN TO THE EXPERTS

I have interviewed at least **two hundred** *experts* in this business; people who make from several hundred thousand a year to over a million dollars a year and more. I took information from each and put it all in one chapter. Read it, please!

It's the "old" way but it's the *certain* way, and you NEED what these people say in order to be successful in Network Marketing. Coupled with my *new* methods, you simply cannot miss!

❏ **BELIEF** in your products, your company, Network Marketing and yourself. When you have this belief, it's easy to share your company with others.

❏ **COMMITMENT** is the key word. Do whatever it takes to get the job done.

❏ **URGENCY** means *push the throttle to the floor,* and have a high level of enthusiasm for an extended period of time so the people around you will feel your energy—your *electricity*—and become a part of it.

❏ **SET YOUR GOALS:** Write them down and read them daily. Dream, and dream BIG! Know the REA-

SONS you want to achieve these goals, WHEN you want to achieve these goals, and HOW you plan to do it. Be specific! Frequently REVIEW these goals.

❏ **DUPLICATION:** This is a word that cannot be overused in Network Marketing. It is **impossible** to succeed alone. Success comes in abundance when you learn the art of duplication. BUILD **a system** that is easily *duplicatable*. **Never do anything other people can't copy!** Have a simple plan, one that everyone can follow, and repeat that plan (that system) over and over and over.

❏ **MAKE A LIST:** Have someone you just sponsored list 20 of the *most important* people in their life, never prejudging anyone. (YOU do the same when you first start). From that list of 20 names, select the **top five** prospects and set an appointment with each for a *two–on–one* presentation or a *three–way* call.

For the presentation, the upline (or mentor) conducts it while you observe. These beginning few prospects are the KEYS to your business. If it's a three–way call, the upline still makes the presentation to the prospect and you listen.

Two things are happening: First, the upline will be more successful with the prospect because they *know* the system. Second, you are being trained. Repeat this procedure until you feel confident to conduct a presentation yourself.

Invite the remaining people to an in-home presentation where the upline looks for the prospects who have *fire in their eyes*, those who recognize the opportunity before them. These potential prospects become the new recruits and the process starts over again, with the former new distributor being the mentor/presenter. This is **DUPLICATION**!

AFTER you finish with the original 20-people, create an *Organic Prospect List* of maybe 200 (neighbors, friends, relatives, acquaintances across the United States or anywhere in the world). Each week, select *ten names* from the list and make these your contact people for the week.

Every week add *five names* to the list, people you meet just walking through life. And remember, NEVER prejudge. You never know who will or who won't be your next leader. If you have but ten new distributors using the same system, after ten weeks you, personally, would have contacted 100 people and if the distributors you trained were trained well, they will have contacted a THOUSAND people! **THIS IS DUPLICATION!** This is the BIG SECRET of what makes Network Marketing work!

❏ **A FOLLOW-UP SYSTEM:** Develop a *follow-up system* for your new distributors and for your retail customers. Send them a tape, a BOOK, any piece of literature for a period of time on a regular basis.

This will introduce them to the entire product *line* a product at a time, or to the business opportunity. It is a very effective *drip system* that leads to building great business relationships as well as bringing steady increases and consistency to your sales.

❏ **A SUPPORT TEAM:** What a fun way to do business. Everyone needs a friend, a cheerleader, a *confidante* in the business. When you are UP, it's great to be recognized, and when you're DOWN, you'll welcome support. Develop a team of four or five people and create a Support Team.

❏ **TEAMWORK:** *Everyone working together* will accomplish more. Be a leader in your business. Remember, you are working WITH your distributors not FOR them. Everyone is in business FOR themselves but not BY themselves. Understanding that each person has different talents allows your distributors to use *their* talents; you will all benefit. If you find a leader, *let them lead!*

❏ **FOCUS:** It's like MAGIC, and gives you a chance for great success in everything you do, and *especially* in Network Marketing. Focus on ONE company. Rarely can you work two or more successfully. There ARE exceptions, of course. If want to build confidence in your distributors, the best way to destroy it is to become the mayor, sheriff, fire chief and postmaster.

❏ **VISION:** This is the initial step to take in creating the business to which you aspire. Tell your distributors, "*If you could only see what I see.*" Remember Helen Keller? She said, "*The most pathetic person in the world is someone who has sight but no vision.*"

Network Marketing has given financial security

to so many. And you, as a leader, can make a positive difference in many lives and represent all that is good about democracy. It gives the average person the *opportunity* or *freedom* to pursue their dreams and to be the best they possibly can be.

This is not a *free lunch* program. It's an *opportunity* to build an organization with hard work and dedication and make money to whatever heights you can imagine.

## ANOTHER EXPERT GIVES ADVICE

As you earn money, get better tools, like a quality telephone with a good answering machine. Get two telephone lines—and 3-way calling. Use the other as a dedicated fax line. Better YET, get a COMPUTER. It is not an instrument of the **future**, it's here NOW. Don't fight it; I did. It's wondrous. It will save you TIME and get your messages out in seconds. It is no longer a luxury or a status symbol, it is a necessary *tool.*

Always have business cards or company and product brochures to hand out, with your name, address and telephone number listed.

Buy as many audio tapes as you can afford, to hand out to those you prospect.

Be smart and **USE THIS BOOK!** It's a *fantastic* marketing tool; the best I've ever seen.

Whether you are a newcomer or a veteran in Network

Marketing, each company has their own *systems* that you must learn. To be successful you have to become a student again.

### *Part 1, The Student*

Because the human mind is so strong-willed and egotistical, one of the greatest challenges for any successful network marketer is to **break all of your old work habits that weren't successful.**

There are new ways that you must learn. You absolutely *must* become a student of these new ways and, try them ALL!

The Network Marketing industry is growing so fast that it's often difficult to comprehend. There are 350,000 people EACH WEEK who are going into a home-based business.

The reasons are: layoffs, downsizing, hostile takeovers, bad management, competition, forced retirement, or just wanting to supplement income. Want to learn this business? Become a student.

> *Study your product line*
> *Study your company*
> *Study the industry of Network Marketing*

It's not easy to be self-motivated, to work when it's more fun to play. But, it takes *money* to play. And, if you firmly believe in something and try to tell others about it, it's difficult to smile when you can see that they do *not* believe in what you fervently believe in.

One of the biggest reasons a person is **not** successful in Network Marketing is *their inability to handle rejection.* You can overcome this by study, by learning the answers, by learning to *counter* rejection. *Then*, rejection becomes a challenge, even fun.

Not *everyone* will listen to you; not *everyone* will buy what you have to sell; not *everyone* is bright enough to know a good opportunity when they see one. That's what I love about the book ideas Pete lists; you don't SELL, you only TELL. It truly works!

Another thing many new people in the business do is to spend hours and DAYS behind the computer trying to **reword** or **restructure** what is written and designed by *marketing experts.* Trust the fact, unless you're an advertising or marketing genius, the company literature is far better than what YOU can do. Just work *their* system!

Pete, with this book, went one step *beyond*! He didn't try to change or rewrite any *company* literature, he created an entirely **new method** in Network Marketing. When I told him it was brilliant, he smiled and agreed.

I think one of the first qualifications for Network Marketing is if you LIKE PEOPLE because this is a *people* business. Hand out company brochures. Take what your sponsor has offered you as far as tools and systems and *go ballistic!* I did and it worked for me. It'll work for you too.

## *Part 2, The Mentor*

A MENTOR is an individual with a proven track record in the field in which you are planning to study. A mentor is someone you want to *mirror,* and by drawing from their wisdom and success you will make fewer mistakes.

The feeling I get is almost indescribable when I see someone that I trained and motivated become successful in Network Marketing. My heart swells with pride as I watch them grow and mature in their own home-based business and then go out and help and teach others to do the same.

Network Marketing has changed my life so dramatically—and it can change yours. It happens to everyone who listens and learns in this business. We, in the industry, refer to it as your *learning curve,* the metamorphosis you go through from student to mentor. This can be a frightening transformation for some, going from a *sponge* for information and knowledge to the one who now teaches.

This puts you in a fish bowl; it means that you are being watched, criticized, emulated, called upon to show others how to duplicate your habits—good and bad. It also means that your *organization* is growing, and as they look upon you for leadership, the responsibility is solely on your shoulders.

TIME MANAGEMENT has been mentioned a time or two in this book, and it is such an *important* work habit to teach as a good mentor. Whether you work your business part-time of full-time, you have only 24 hours to account for in each day.

If you manage your time *poorly*, it will consume you and offers little reward. A good mentor should be able to scan through their organization and spot the *rising* stars. Spend a large majority of your time with these people and both of your businesses will grow faster as a result. Here's why.

In Network Marketing (possibly any business) **20% of the people do 80% of the sales volume**. So, if you spend *most of your time* with that 20%, you are working smart! For those of you who want to make millions, don't WASTE time trying get others to "see the picture." If they do, work with them and if not, PASS THEM UP! Sometimes we want success for our associate more than the associate wants success for themselves. That will never work; *you can't push a rope.* You must **sponsor** *for potential, but get* **excited** *over results.*

Work with are the ones who want success as much (or almost as much) as YOU want it. And as a coach and mentor, it is your responsibility to show this new student the real BIG PICTURE of Network Marketing. Tell them that it takes study, and learning, and teaching, and *time*; it can't all happen in a month; it might take a year, or two, or three.

Don't let me *frighten* you with this statement. I don't mean you'll starve during this time, quite the contrary. Just that the **BIG** money comes when you have a large organization and no matter how fast you are, it just takes time.

*Oh,* you'll still be living well if you work and teach, but to really get rich, it just takes T-I-M-E. Show me what other business you can get in and start at the very bottom, with absolutely no prior training, and earn $100,000 to $1,000,000 or more the first year!

A smart mentor must also try to get their new associate a check **quickly**. If they don't reach a certain level of success in the first three months, either of three things usually happen:

✳     *You lose them forever.*
✳     *They quit and look for another Network Marketing company.*
✳     *They will give Network Marketing a bad rap. It isn't entirely their fault, you have to accept part of the blame, also.*

That's why it's up to you, as mentor, to see that *realistic* goals are set, *systems* followed, and proper *work habits are* drilled in their heads. You must *coach* them every step of the way. It is up to you to teach them the *mechanics* of Network Marketing. It will, undoubtedly, make YOU rich!

Stay *by their side* for their first 30 phone calls. Join *them* on their first 10 appointments. Conduct their first several interviews until your student learns to do it themselves.

By doing this, you will have an excited *student* on your hands. As they go through their *learning curve,* your business is growing as their's grows. If you are programming your time, you will have several students in training at the same time.

## AUTHORS CLOSING COMMENTS

This wasn't so bad, was it? Learn anything? I certainly hope so. TRY Network Marketing as a home-based business PART TIME; if you work for it and it works for you, it truly is YOUR CHANCE to change your lifestyle and that of your kids and grandkids FOREVER!

This book is ONLY for those who want to have an OPPORTUNITY to work for themselves. Don't retire FROM something, retire TO something. Have a job? KEEP IT until you are confident that this new home-based business works.

Is it HARD work to become rich? **YES!** Is Network Marketing for everybody? **NO!** Is it GUARAN-TEED to make you successful? **OF COURSE NOT!** (Most people fail at *whatever* they do.) Can you do it? **PROBABLY!** (You won't know if you don't try.)

Remember, **"IF YOU DON'T TAKE A CHANCE, YOU'LL NEVER HAVE A CHANCE."** Just be smart about it; choose the product, the company, the pay plan, and KNOW that it is NOT easy work.

However, working for yourself in your own HOME-BASED BUSINESS is a CHANCE to get rich and, MANY are doing it.

# ABOUT THE AUTHOR

PETE BILLAC is one of the most sought-after speakers in the United States. This is his 50<sup>th</sup> book; 44 have become BEST-SELLERS. His worldwide best seller, HOW NOT TO BE LONELY, sold over FIVE million copies. His books are published in 31 languages.

Pete is a maverick; he writes what pleases him. His topics range from adventure to war, the Mafia, famous people, to romance, love, health, and motivation.

He speaks to Fortune 500 companies on marketing, he lectures at universities across America, and delivers his "message" at conventions and seminars around the world. For fun, he conducts lectures on cruise ships.

Pete is currently traveling the world with his newest book, *THE NEW MILLIONAIRES*. "*This book, tells people how to realize their potential and get out of their financial quagmire. Making money is great—and easy, too, if you believe in yourself and work smart. God wants you to be prosperous, and to help others along the way.*"

Perhaps you've seen Pete on Donahue, Sally Jessy Raphael, Good Morning America, Laff Stop or other national televison shows. He mixes common sense and knowledge with laughter. He charms his audiences with his quick wit and candor, and breathes life into every topic. He makes his audiences laugh—hard!

*"Pete is an expert at restoring self-confidence and self-esteem in others . . ."*

**Phil Donahue**
**National Television Talk Show Host**

# *The* New Millionaires

## Swan Publishing

**Southwind Ranch**
**1059 CR 100**
**Burnet, TX   78611**
*To contact Pete:*
**Call (512) 756-6800**
**Fax  (512) 756-0102**

*Visit our web site at:* http:\\www.swan-pub.com

**For your FREE Info Packet for RADIO, email:**
**swanbooks@ghg.net**

## FOR MORE INFORMATION CALL:

## YOUR sticker here!

*After reading this book, please pass it on to a friend or relative. It could change their financial lives forever!*